THE WIRRAL COUN
By TB Maund

GW01185950

A Leyland charabanc operated by Hardings, then located at Charing Cross,
Birkenhead, is shown on a party outing about 1919. [Hardings (Wirral) Ltd].

Design & Origination: Ian Boumphrey – Desk Top Publisher

Printed by: Bookprint Sl, Barcelona

Published by: Ian & Marilyn Boumphrey 'The Nook' 7 Acrefield Road Prenton Wirral CH42 8LD
Tel/Fax: 0151 608 7611
E-mail: ian@yesterdayswirral.co.uk
Web Site: www.yesterdayswirral.co.uk

FRONT COVER

Top: *The Leyland Titan TD1 model could be seen in Crosville service in Birkenhead for 24 years - from 1929 to 1953. This
one, seen parked out of service in Beckwith Street, adjoining Birkenhead Park station entered service as No.48 in
1931, became L10 in the 1935 renumbering and, eventually M160 when fitted with a diesel engine. Note the post-war
prefabricated house to the left, one of hundreds erected after the 1939-45 war to ease the shortage of housing caused
by enemy bombing.* (TB Maund collection)
Middle: *Crosville charabanc outside the* Plough Inn *Moreton – see page 14*
Bottom: *John Pye Bus No.8 – see page 17*

ISBN 1-899241-23-X

Price
£6.95

THE WIRRAL COUNTRY BUS

INTRODUCTION

From early in the 20th century private individuals and companies were exploring the possibilities of linking the outlying Wirral villages with the principal towns of Birkenhead and Wallasey by means of the motor bus. Others provided charabancs to give the inhabitants of the towns the opportunities to see the countryside for pleasure purposes; these were crude solid-tyred vehicles and minimum protection from the rain but a ride was still sufficient of a novelty for the discomforts to be treated as part of the adventure. Prior to the 1914-18 War motor vehicles tended to be unreliable but wartime needs led to a great improvement in performance and reliability and the aftermath provided a huge pool of both army surplus vehicles at low prices and men who had been trained to drive and maintain them.

Although the first Crosville bus ran from Chester to Ellesmere Port in 1911 and the Chester-New Ferry service along the main road started in 1913, the war prevented any further significant developments until 1919. Even though the peninsula was well provided with railways, the almost door-to-door nature of bus travel had an instant appeal, especially in villages such as Greasby, Frankby Pensby and Barnston which were remote from a railway station. Whilst these places are now regarded as dormitory suburbs, they were very much in the country then and it was the bus which stimulated their growth by providing cheap and reliable transport.

But the early bus operators had a formidable hurdle to surmount and that was the hostility of the local councils, particularly Birkenhead and Wallasey, who had invested large sums in municipal tramways the revenue base of which they were determined to protect at all costs. Others, particularly Hoylake and West Kirby, were obstructive on the grounds of protecting amenities or for religious reasons. Wartime legislation in 1916 enabled councils to impose mileage charges on bus operators inaugurating new services because of the damage it was alleged they caused. This was highly discriminatory as much heavier vehicles including road locomotives and steam wagons paid no such charge. These charges were abolished after the Roads Act 1920 introduced road fund licensing for all mechanical vehicles.

The larger authorities had the power to license vehicles and their drivers and conductors plying for hire under the Town Police Clauses Acts, 1847 and 1889, legislation clearly designed for horse-drawn traffic. Buses were not allowed to penetrate to town centres but were required to decant their passengers at a tram terminus to continue their journeys in an Edwardian tramcar. Some councillors were sufficiently far-sighted to recognise that the buses would bring in passengers who would spend money in the town and this sometimes led to conflict within councils, some members objecting to the hard line taken by the Tramways Committee. The Roads Act 1920, which established the Ministry of Transport, provided an appeal procedure against refusal of a licence, but not against the constant adjournments and delays practised by some councils. It was not until 1931, following the passing of the Road Traffic Act, 1930, that road service licensing became a national matter in the hands of Traffic Commissioners.

The buses of the original Crosville Motor Co., founded in 1906, were restricted to termini at New Ferry, Prenton tram terminus in Prenton Road West, and Singleton Avenue. The most outrageous of all was Bidston Hill Waterworks, a steep climb from the nearest tram at Claughton Village. Although Crosville was able to gain access to Birkenhead Park station in 1924 the other restrictions remained in place until 1930 except for the exploitation of a loophole in the law which enabled them to run buses to Woodside for prepaid contract-holders only. Wallasey restricted Crosville buses to a terminus in Wallasey Village at the top of Leasowe Road; an appeal to the Minister of Transport enabled them to extend to the Queen's Arms Hotel, Liscard Village in April 1925 but they never managed to penetrate to New Brighton. In retrospect, it is clear that the Crosville management of the time was dilatory in pressing their case and actually negotiated away their right to appeal to the Minister of Transport .

In 1929 Crosville was purchased outright by the London, Midland & Scottish Railway (LMS) the management of which brought pressure to bear on the intransigent authorities including Birkenhead. This resulted in a formal Agreement being drawn up establishing the spheres of influence of Crosville and Birkenhead Corporation buses. Nevertheless Crosville paid a high price to reach Woodside as passengers could not be set down before arrival at Allport Road, Bromborough, Upton Cricket Ground, Rosclare Drive, Moreton and the point at which Landican Cemetery gates now stand. Services were extended from the outlying termini to Woodside in two stages on 1st August and 1st October 1930 and Birkenhead Corporation buses were extended to Eastham, Irby, Thurstaston and Heswall and later on to Clatterbridge, Greasby and Frankby. In the meantime in May 1930 the LMS Railway which had changed the livery of the buses from the original drab grey to the maroon worn by their railway carriages, had sold half its interest in Crosville to Tilling and British Automobile Traction Co. Ltd. and a new company, Crosville Motor Services Ltd. was formed. The extension of country bus routes into town centres brought an enormous increase in traffic and further growth in the outlying districts. In 1942 the Tilling and British Automobile holding company was divided into separate Tilling and BET Groups leaving Crosville in the former. This resulted in a further change of livery from maroon to green though, under wartime conditions, it took a few years before all buses were repainted. The Wirral Country Bus achieved the peak of its prosperity by the 1950s after which the spread of television killed the profitable evening traffic and the proliferation of private transport led to a general decline in bus use which has continued ever since.

In this book the role played by the private charabanc and coach operators in opening up the countryside has not been overlooked. Annual outings were enjoyed by Church groups, clubs and pubs and public excursions to beauty spots, race meetings, football matches etc. were well patronised. Some of these operators developed their excursions into daily, time-tabled express services, particularly to North Wales resorts. All these and the London services, which first ran in 1928, finished up in the hands of Crosville.

The selection of pictures includes no modern views, ending approximately in the 1960s.

TICKETS

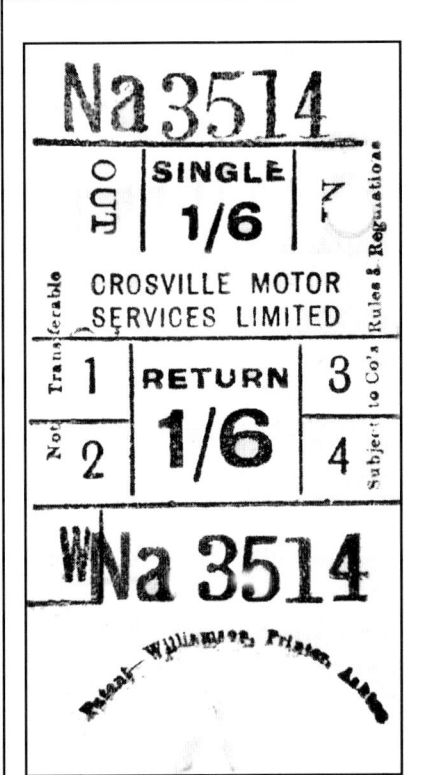

In the days before tickets were issued from machines, separate different coloured tickets were printed for each value, made up into bundles of 100 and carried by conductors in wooden racks. On the longer services, Crosville conductors needed a great many different tickets and sometimes carried two ticket racks. The 1/6d ticket, punched for a single journey, was the price of a journey from Chester to Woodside. It was coloured pale pink. For a return fare, the ticket would be punched in the lower section and, on the return journey, the top would be torn off and an exchange ticket issued.

Under the 1930 Agreement with Birkenhead Corporation, Crosville was permitted to issue through tickets to Liverpool via Woodside ferry, a facility which the Corporation buses had had since 1928. This dark grey 1/4d (7.5p) ticket could be used on the return journey on either a Crosville or a Corporation bus.

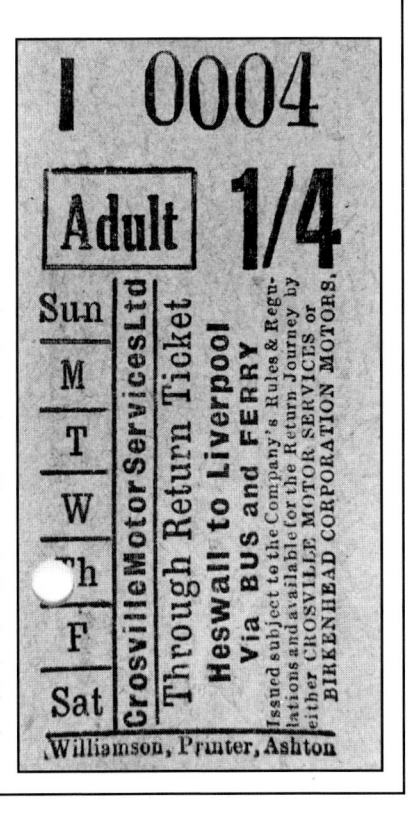

1/2. The Crosville service between New Ferry and Chester by the main road started on 25th January 1913 and a local photographer was there to record the event. In the upper picture the bus was emerging from New Ferry Road on to New Chester Road; it was one of nine Lacres owned by the company, FM 469. Crosville buses were originally named and this one was *The Royal George*, later becoming No. 3, the body having been built by Eaton, a Manchester firm. The lower picture shows the same vehicle on a different occasion in Bromborough village. It is believed to have survived until 1927.   (TB Maund collection)

3/4. An unlikely bus operator was Sir William Lever, the Port Sunlight industrialist who, in 1914, decided to provide a service for his tenants and estate workers in Raby, Thornton Hough, Brimstage and Storeton. A service ran between Raby and Prenton tram terminus in Prenton Road West, near the corner of Storeton Road. Little information his survived about this service but it is known that there were two buses, a Star and an Alldays & Onions and that it continued to run during the war, a gas bag being fitted to one of the buses to beat the petrol shortage. Sir William asked the Wirral Rural District Council to do some tree-lopping to make clearance for this bag as so many of the estate workers had joined the armed services. To some extent the buses used the tree-lined private roads on the estate and during the war were driven by women with youths acting as conductors. The gates on the private roads were kept locked and the conductor alighted to open each one, locking it again after the bus had passed through. It is not known why the service was withdrawn in 1918.

The upper picture shows the Star bus standing outside New Ferry tram depot and it seems that it was used to convey key workers to the outlying factories at Bromborough Port during the war. Levers had no fewer than 19 Star vans (M 1951-69) and it is possible that this was one of them with a different body. The origins of the Birmingham firm of Alldays and Onions who manufactured the bus in the lower picture go back as far as 1625! They made a wide variety of products including bellows and foundry equipment and diversified into cycles, motor cycles, cars and commercial vehicles but these never became the mainstay of their production. It still exists as Alldays, Peacock & Co. making industrial fans in Weston-super-Mare. It is not certain that the vehicle in the lower picture was the Lever bus but it was of this type, seating about 26 passengers. Only one vehicle of this make has been found in Cheshire County Council registration records (M 3955) but there is no proof that it was Lever's bus.   (TB Maund collection)

5/6/7 The Birkenhead firm of Harding's originated in 1891 and engaged in both coach operation and furniture removing. In the upper picture a horse-drawn waggonette, loaded with passengers, stands outside Park Entrance at Birkenhead. The second picture shows a very high built Leyland charabanc CM 593, known to have been owned by Alfred Harding by 1916, on the 1919 Annual Picnic of Cammell Laird's woodworking machinists. This was based on a goods chassis and may have had a lorry body for use during the week. Next, a group of Harding's charabancs is seen at the Cat and Fiddle Inn, between Macclesfield and Buxton and over 1,000 ft above sea-level, a testing climb for vehicles of this vintage. The small one on the left was a Vulcan and most, if not all, the others were Leylands. (RL Wilson collection)

8. The New Brighton Motor Coach Co. Ltd., formed in 1914, was renowned for its pristine white Daimler charabancs. Based in Grosvenor Road, New Brighton, it had a strong following from local organisations and also ran day and half-day excursions from New Brighton promenade. In the first picture, a party filling five vehicles was photographed in Mill Lane, Liscard outside the water tower, probably about 1919-20. The coach nearest the camera is HF 773.

9. The second view shows a military party at Chester Castle, the small coach on the right, probably a 14 or 16 seater, being HF 73.

10. Members of the New Brighton Improvements Association occupy three coaches, HF 819, 669 and 671) on an outing to Betws-y-Coed in the third view.

11. Lastly, the New Brighton Motor Coach Co. was unfortunate to take delivery of these two Daimler CBs, HF 145, 147, just before the outbreak of war in 1914. Crosville, who had been given the responsibility of transporting workers to a munitions factory at Queensferry, was pleased to take them off their hands in 1916 and they became Nos. 19 (later 37) and 20, remaining in the fleet until 1930 and 1927 respectively.

(TG Turner collection)

12. In the upper view, two Daimler charabancs of the New Brighton Motor Coach Co. are seen outside the firm's head office and garage in Grosvenor Road, New Brighton. Two of their Daimler charabancs, fitted with pneumatic tyres, stand with their hoods raised against the rain.

13. The lower picture shows Daimler HF 115, dating from 1913-14 outside the Convalescent Home in the lower part of Rowson Street. This building later became the Maris Stella Girls' High School which was demolished many years ago to make way for new housing.

14. This picture was taken at Seacombe ferry beside the shelter-cum-cabmen's refuge which stood in the centre of the ferry approach until 1933. This seems to be a school party. Note the white-walled pneumatic tyres and the six separate doors, one to each row of seats.

15. The lower picture shows the smallest Daimler charabanc mounted on a modified limousine chassis. These would seat 12-14 passengers and were quite economic in their day. Note the wire wheels and spare wheel strapped to the side.
   (TG Turner collection)

16. The Crosville service from West Kirby to Wallasey Village started on 28th July 1920. At first the buses ran up St. John's Road to meet the trams in St. George's Road but this soon ceased and buses turned at the top of Leasowe Road. The company had sought to run to New Brighton, Egremont and Seacombe ferries but the Corporation, described by the Area Manager as the most difficult one he had to deal with, refused permission. It was only after an appeal to the Minister of Transport that the buses were allowed to run to the Queen's Arms Hotel, Liscard Village from 13th April 1925 immediately after Wallasey Village, St. Hilary Brow and Wallasey Road had been reconstructed to an acceptable standard. The first view shows a close-up of the front of Daimler CK No. 41 with 23-seat Bartle body carrying a board inscribed 'Service 22 Wallasey-Moreton-Kirby' (sic). The bus was new in 1920 and the occasion may have been the opening of the service.

17/18. The second picture shows a Leyland bus at the top of Leasowe Road, looking west. Note the branch of Irwins, a well-known grocery chain whose red and cream tiled shops could be found all over north Wirral until the 1950s. Lastly an unidentified all-Leyland GH7, new in 1923, makes its way up a rather quiet Leasowe Road to Wallasey Village. St Hilary's church stands high on the right.   (TG Turner collection)

19.   Crosville No. 108, a long wheelbase Leyland 36GH7 40-seater, new in 1923 stops in Reeds Lane, Leasowe with the Castle in the background. The Wallasey-West Kirby service was very popular, justifying the allocation of the largest vehicles then available.   (TG Turner collection)

20/21.   Following the success of the West Kirby-Wallasey Village service in 1920, Crosville people spent the winter planning full coverage of north Wirral, a number of new services starting on 5th May 1921. One of these was the 'Wirral Outer Circle', for which the summer and winter 1922 timetables are shown here. Note that in the winter, apart from one trip round the circle in each direction, it was demoted to a Caldy-Meols local service. The Circle was not a success and was replaced in 1923 by separate services over each section of route.   (TB Maund collection)

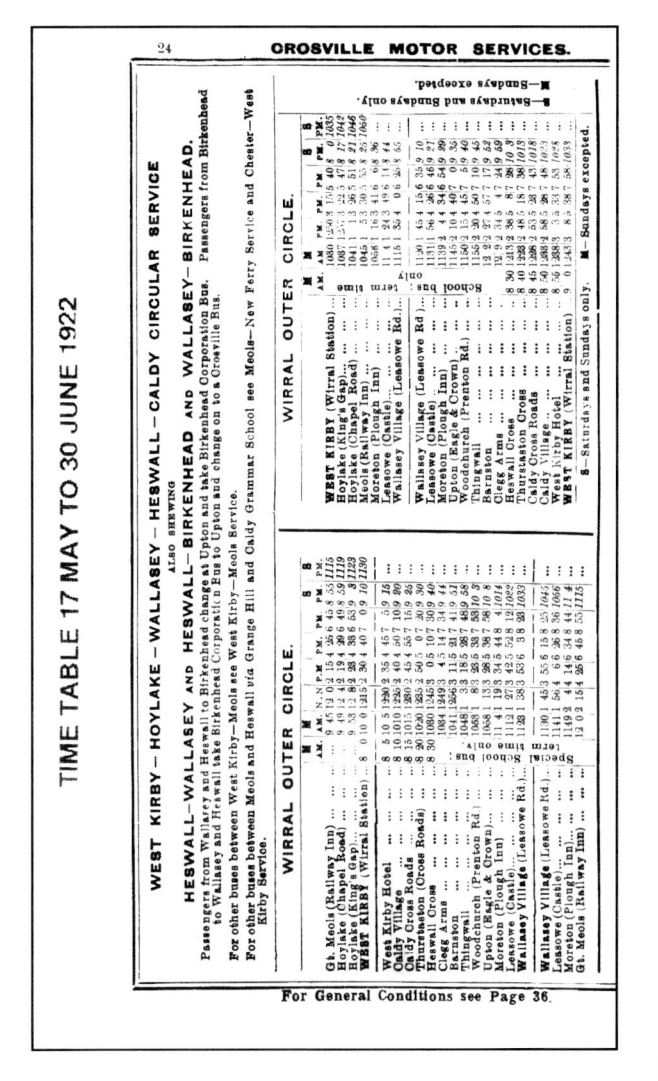

22/23. This further view of *The Royal George* when new and *The Flying Fox* at New Ferry Toll Bar are of interest as they show the unusual open rear platform of the Eaton bodies, the statutory 12 mph speed limit sign and the fully opening windscreen. On the original print it is possible to discern on the ruby toplight ventilators advertisements for Crosville cars and accessories, repairs, tyres, petrol and oils, another facet of the company's activities at that time.
(TB Maund collection)

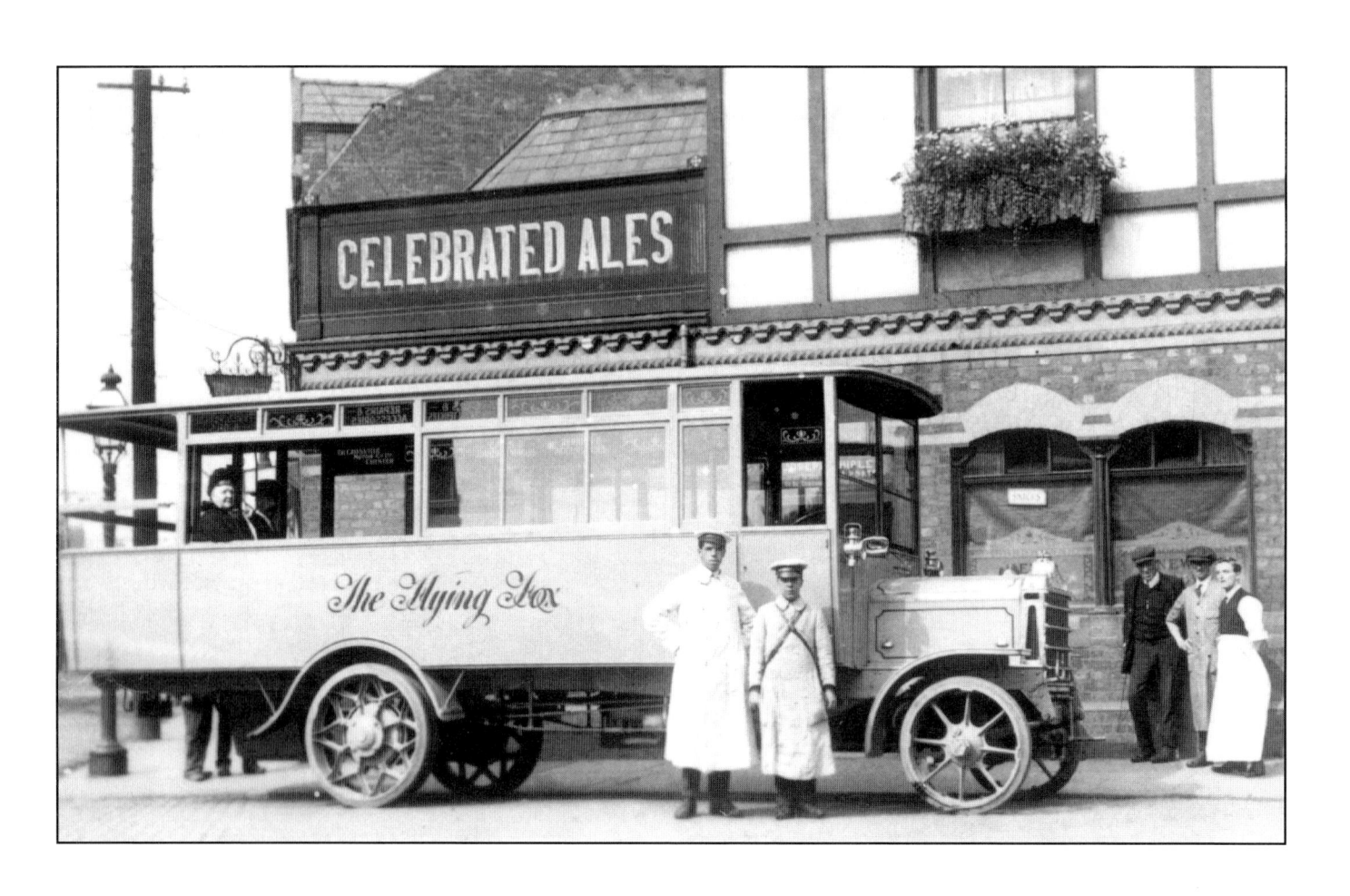

24/25. Two views of the Toll Bar, New Ferry illustrate the artificial barrier erected by Birkenhead Corporation in denying Crosville access to central Birkenhead. In the upper picture 1921 Daimler CK FM 2044 (No. 60) is exiting New Ferry Road whilst a 1911 Hurst Nelson tram which has brought its passengers from Birkenhead waits its time to return to Woodside. Below an older tram connects with a newer bus. On the left one of the original 1901 Milnes single-deck trams with a special top deck added, low enough to go beneath Chester Street bridge, feeds a half-cab bus, probably a 1925 Leyland SG9.

(TG Turner collection)

CROSVILLE

MOTOR SERVICES.
CHESTER, ELLESMERE PORT & NEW FERRY,
COMBINED SERVICES.

TIME TABLES AND FARES UNTIL FURTHER NOTICE.

Services 3 & 6   From Chester to Ellesmere Port and New Ferry   1, 2, 19

(timetable and fares table)

Telephone 268.   PROPRIETORS: The Crosville Motor Co., Ltd., Crane Wharf, Chester.

Form 26. 5,000. 11/1/19.   Motor Buses and Open Char-a-bancs for Private Hire.   *Taberer, Printer, Chester*

26. A Crosville timetable dated 11th January 1919 probably advertised the first post-1914-18 war increase in services between New Ferry and Chester. Note that, except on Saturdays and Sundays, the last bus from Chester ran at 6.0 pm and from New Ferry at 7.15 pm. The journey took one hour by the direct route and 1hr 10min via Ellesmere Port for a fare of 1s.7d (8p). In the 1930s the fare from Woodside to Chester was 1s 6d single or 2s.0d (10p) return.

(TB Maund collection)

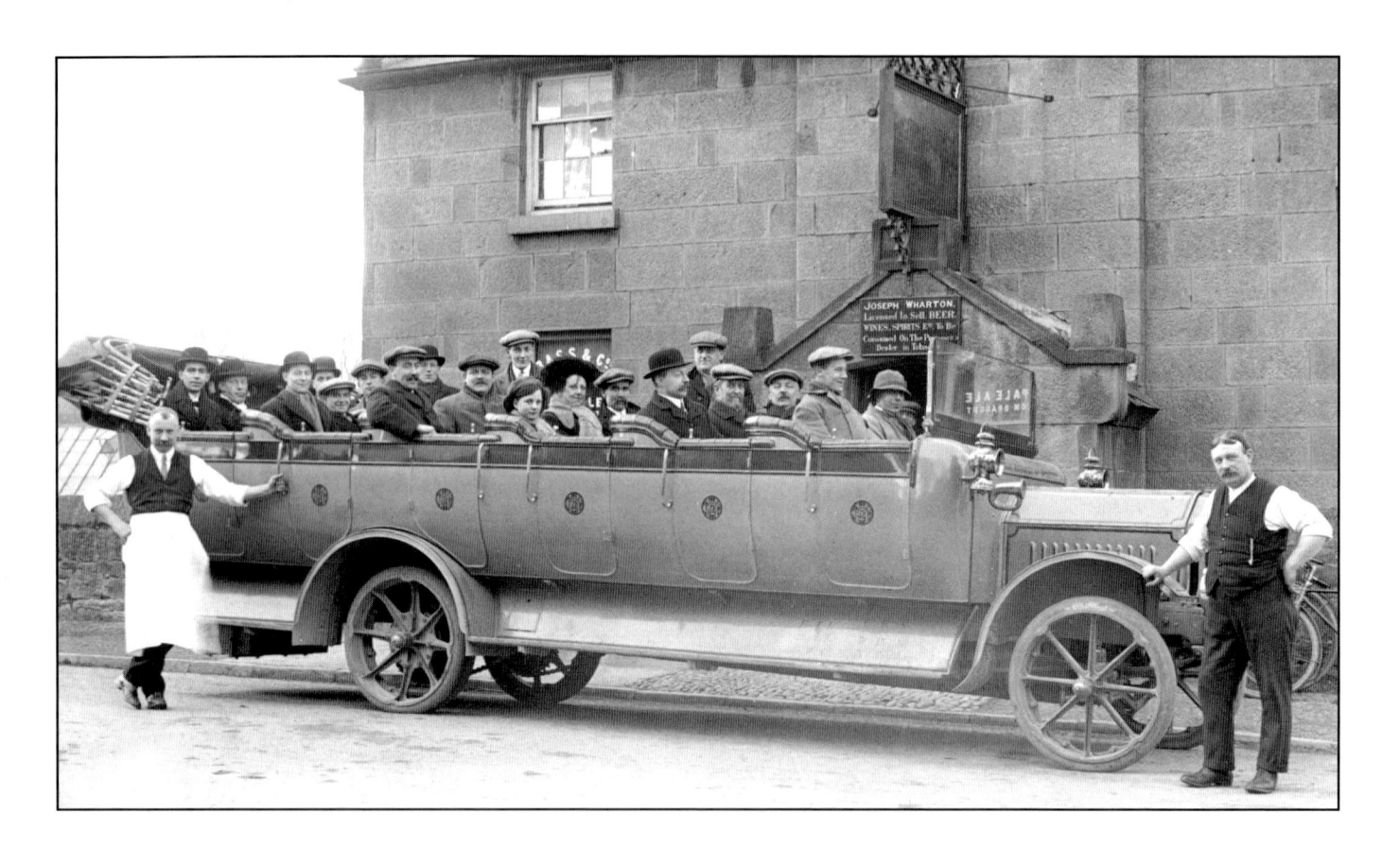

27/28/29. Crosville had its share of charabancs and the Hoylake & West Kirby Council allocated three stands, at West Kirby Wirral station, King's Gap and Hoyle Road but steadfastly refused to allow their use on Sundays, potentially the most profitable day. The upper picture shows a Lacre at the old Plough Inn at Moreton with the landlord, Joe Wharton, on the right. This sandstone building was demolished in the early 1930s and the new Plough Inn was erected on the site. The vehicle was probably FM 535, an 18-seater which was named *Grey Knight* when new. The lower picture is of Crosville No.12 with canvas roof in position. This had a short life with the company and, although almost certainly soon fitted with pneumatic tyres, was sold in 1928 by which time the traditional charabanc design was regarded as distinctly dated. The same vehicle, pictured opposite, leads a convoy on what appears to be a women's outing.
(I & M Boumphrey/Crosville/TG Turner collection)

30.   This post 1914-18 War shot of Chester Market Square shows seven Crosville buses, all of Daimler or Lacre manufacture. The buses from New Ferry and Ellesmere Port terminated here.   (TB Maund collection)

31.   West Kirby Wirral station with two Crosville Leylands, the one on the right being a 36GH7 No.77 which ran from 1922 to 1928. The main stop was near the Dee Hotel where passengers boarded buses on the wrong side of the road, a practice which was not ended until 1942 when it was discontinued because of the wartime blackout.
    (I & M Boumphrey)

32/33. There were two private firms in Moreton running buses or coaches. J W Bell had a long history and the upper picture is of interest because of the comparative rarity of the makes of charabanc depicted. On the left is NB 8132, a Caledon as indicated by the saltire on the radiator tank whilst NB 7355 is a Palladium. Cole's 'Dinky Bus', a Ford Model T, was mainly used for a service between Moreton Cross and the Embankment as Moreton Shore was called in those days, at a fare of 1d (½d for a child). Both Birkenhead Corporation and Crosville fought over this route, the latter with an open charabanc on fine days and Cole was put out of business in the late 1920s

(TB Maund collection)

34. The best known of the small operators in Wirral was John Pye of Heswall who started running buses between Heswall and the corner of Singleton Avenue and Borough Road, Birkenhead in 1919. That was as far as Birkenhead Corporation would allow him to go, passengers being required to transfer to a tram to get into town. Because of the roundabout railway route via Hooton and the distance of Heswall station from much of the residential area, the service was a great success and the original route through Pensby was supplemented by buses running via Thurstaston and Irby and via Barnston. Pye had a very mixed fleet with ten makes in a fleet of 21 buses. The Albion No.8, registered MA 8259 was one of his earliest.
(TB Maund collection)

35. Pye built a bus station at the bottom of Singleton Avenue and his solitary Pagefield, No. 5, MA 4067, is seen standing outside. Note the tram stop sign on the pole just behind the front of the bus. Pagefields were built by Walkers at Wigan and there were several at work in Birkenhead and Liverpool as 'piggy-back' lorries for horse-drawn refuse carts. (TB Maund collection)

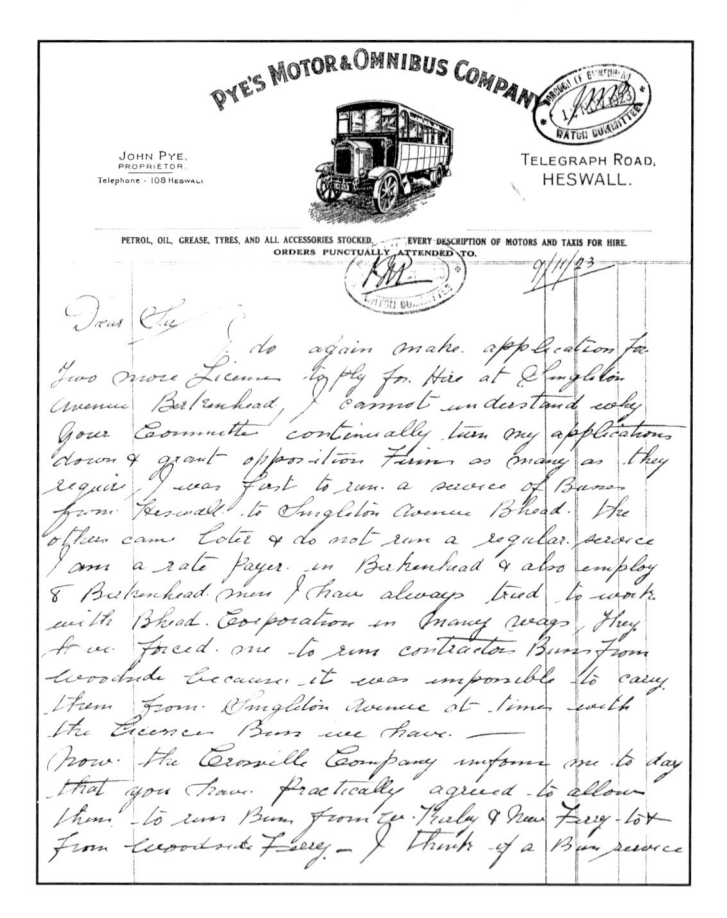

36/37. Pye was badly treated by Birkenhead Watch Committee who refused to issue sufficient licences to enable him to cater for the traffic. Eventually he exploited a loophole in the law whereby vehicles on which no fares were collected were not deemed as plying for hire. Contracts and prepaid tickets were sold and buses without Birkenhead licences were run through to Woodside during the morning and evening peak hours. The letter shown was one written to the Town Clerk on 9th November 1923 pleading for more licences. Also shown is a bus licence issued on 16th July 1923 for Straker Squire No.10 (MA 9642) ;the 'special conditions' were the prohibition of the picking up or setting down of passengers within six miles of Singleton Avenue, an absurd and unenforceable rule as the borough boundary at that time was near the Half Way House.

(T B Maund collection)

38. A much altered winter time-table for Pye's service dating from 1922 or 1923 appeared on the reverse of the picture of the Pagefield bus illustrated above.

(TB Maund collection)

County Borough of Birkenhead.

OMNIBUSES, WAGGONETTES, & OTHER CARRIAGES.

CARRIAGE LICENSE.

No. 121
M.A. 9642

The Mayor, Aldermen and Burgesses of the Borough of Birkenhead acting by the Council of the said Borough, under and by virtue of the provisions of the Town Police Clauses Act, 1847, the Public Health Act, 1875, and the Birkenhead Corporation Act, 1881. and in pursuance of a requisition duly made to them in accordance with the said Acts, DO HEREBY LICENSE a four wheeled Carriage, commonly called an *Omnibus* to ply for hire as a Motor Hackney Carriage within the limits of the Borough of Birkenhead, from the 16th day of July 1923 until the First day of July, 1924, under and subject to the Orders, Rules, Regulations, and Bye-laws respecting Omnibuses, Waggonettes, and other Carriages, and the Proprietors and Drivers thereof, from time to time in force, and to the statutes in that behalf made and provided, *and to the special conditions on back hereof*.

Name or Names of Proprietor or Part Proprietor of the Hackney Carriage	Place or Places of Abode
John Pye	Heswall

Given under the Common Seal of the said MAYOR, ALDERMEN and BURGESSES this 15th day of Septr. 1923

Sealed in the presence of

Collins
MAYOR.

(This License must be delivered up to the Inspector of Hackney Carriages on the Annual Inspection Day).

437-829 250 11-20.

TIME TABLE

On and after 1st October. until further notice.

HESWALL. Pye's Garage.			BIRKENHEAD. Singleton Avenue Offices.		
a.m.			a.m.		
7 50			8 30	9 0	
8 30			9 30 B		
9 0 B			~~10 0~~	10 30 T	
Via Hotel ~~9 45~~ T	9 30		~~10 45 T~~	11 30	
10 0			~~11 45~~		
~~10 30 B~~			~~12 45~~ B	12·30	
11 0			1 30		
12 0 B			2 15 T		
12 45			3 0		
1 30 T			3 45		
2 15			4 30		
3 0			~~5 15~~ B	5 0	
3 45			6 0		
4 30 B	5 30		6 30 T		
5 15			~~7 0~~	7 15	
5 45 T			~~7 45~~	8 15 B	
6 30			~~8 30~~		
~~7 0~~ T	7 30		9 15 B		
~~7 45~~			~~10 0~~		
8 30 B			~~10 30~~	10 15	
9 30					
10 30 Tues. and Sats.			11 20 Tues. and Sats.		

B—These Buses travel via Barnston
T—These Buses travel via Thurstaston.

SUNDAYS.

Heswall - - - 9-15, ~~11-30 a.m., 11 p.m. and Hourly~~ until 10 0 p.m.

Birkenhead - - - 10-15 a.m., ~~12-30, 1-30 p.m. and Half~~ past every hour until 10-30 p.m.

Private Buses, Char-a-Bancs and Taxis for Hire

39. John Pye was not the only firm to run between Birkenhead and Heswall. E & J Johnston, trading as Borough Motor Works ran an infrequent service from a yard in Carlton Road by both the Pensby and Irby & Thurstaston routes, using this Leyland charabanc and a 20-seat Daimer bus. Johnston's business was bought by Harding's from 1st October 1924 much to Crosville's chagrin but Alfred Harding sold the goodwill to them and Crosville's monopoly was established from 10th January 1925.

(His Honour Judge McKay)

40. Crosville charabancs were used in fine weather on timetabled summer services to Mold, Loggerheads and North Wales coastal resorts. They were also used locally between Singleton Avenue and Thurstaston and Moreton Cross and the Shore. On some North Wales trips buses from both Singleton Avenue and Wallasey would meet up at Heswall and, if bookings were light, only one would run through. This was a Leyland C1, originally No. 90 but later renumbered 11. It ran from 1923 to 1929. (Crosville)

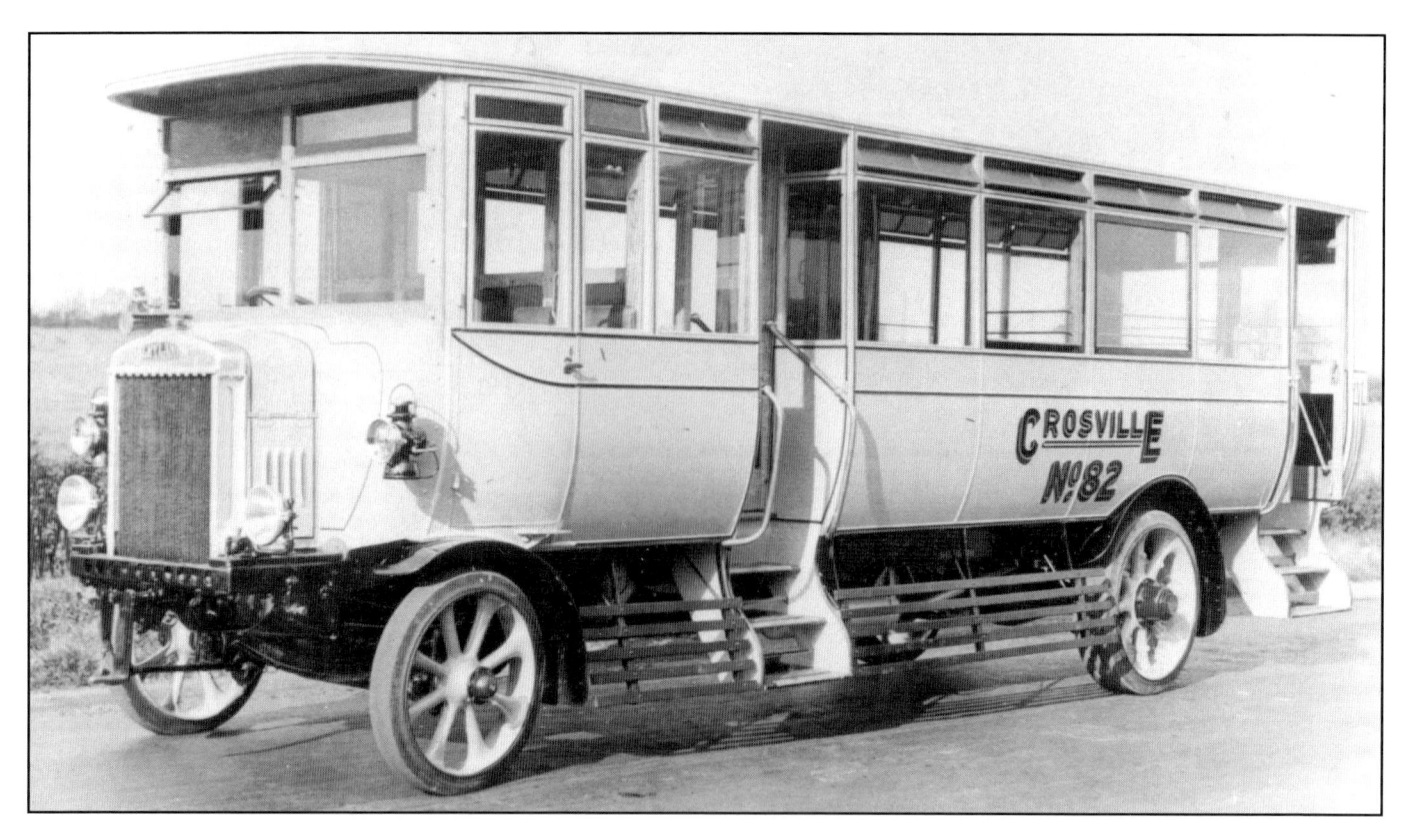

41.   As the services became more popular larger buses were needed and the long-wheelbase version of the Leyland 36SG7 model, with two entrances and 40 seats became a popular crowd-shifter, up to 60 passengers being crammed in on busy Saturday nights. This was the first Leyland model with the engine partly alongside the driver. Note that, to aid steering, the front wheels were smaller than the rears. No.82 (later No.100), new in 1922, was later fitted with pneumatic tyres and finally withdrawn in 1931.

   (RL Wilson collection)

42.   No. 59 was one of the last Daimler CK models to join the fleet being fitted with a 26-seat two-door Bartle body when new in 1920. However 45 Daimlers had new Leyland bodies fitted in 1924 and as tyre technology developed, pneumatic tyres were substituted for solids soon after .In this picture it was parked close to the rear of a Leviathan double-decker in Beckwith Street, Birkenhead opposite Christ the King church, which was Crosville's Park Station terminus until the late 1930s.   The bus is painted in the short-lived bright red livery adopted for a short time in the late 1920s; it was withdrawn in 1931.

   (D S Deacon)

43. An all-Leyland 36C7R which seated 32 passengers, three of them alongside the driver. New in 1925, these buses were fitted with pneumatic tyres from new but were withdrawn as obsolescent in 1932.
(Leyland Motors)

44. On 22nd January 1924 Crosville took over John Pye's Heswall business but was unable to persuade Birkenhead Watch Committee to issue licences to run to Woodside. However the through contractors' buses were increased until there were eventually 28 journeys daily in each direction. Crosville extended Pye's Singleton Avenue premises, adding what became known as the glasshouse. A Leyland PLSC Lion stands at the terminus with a pneumatic-tyred SG in the background. Note the much lower chassis level of the 1928 Lion.
(TB Maund collection)

45/46. Crosville's rural services needed few double-deck buses and the 12 Leyland LG1 Leviathans received in 1926 were the first new buses of the type. All worked in Wirral, mainly from West Kirby and New Ferry though one of two were based at Chester. The Leviathans had a high floor level and slatted wooden seats for 52 passengers. They worked the Wallasey and Birkenhead services from West Kirby and the New Ferry-Bromborough-Eastham local service from New Ferry depot. There were also trips on the New Ferry-Ellesmere Port-Chester services and a definite record of journeys to Stanlow. They were originally finished in the company's rather drab grey livery but with cream upper deck panels. Numbered 211-222, they were never fitted with pneumatic tyres and all were withdrawn as obsolescent in 1931. The upper picture shows Market Street, Hoylake in the late 1920s with a Leviathan double-decker in the grey and cream livery heading for West Kirby from either Liscard or Park Station. The roadside gardens on the left were later sacrificed for road widening. (Lower), Leviathan No. 216, in an experimental red livery, was photographed while parked up at West Kirby between duties.

(Ian Boumphrey/TG Turner collection)

47. Crosville's New Ferry bus station in New Ferry Road, close to the Toll Bar, was a busy place doubling as a garage at night. A Leyland Leviathan is loading, probably on the local service to Bromborough or Eastham. After Crosville's Rock Ferry garage was opened on 1st April 1932, the building was sold and used as a market for some years. Parts of it still exist in a disused state.

(RL Wilson collection)

48. Crosville Daimler CK No. 54 with 26-seat dual-entrance Bartle body was new in 1920 and is seen in Lower Bebington working on the Rock Ferry pier-Raby Mere service which started on 4th June 1924 and ran seasonally until 1938. Crosville offered to sell it to Birkenhead Corporation but the manager, Cyril Clarke, refused saying that there weren't enough passengers to fill a taxi.

(TG Turner collection)

49. Small buses which could be operated by one man were needed for lightly-trafficked services and No.120, a 20-seat Leyland Z5, new in 1924, seems to have been the first Crosville bus to have been delivered new with pneumatic tyres. It also had a jack-knife door controlled by a lever and buses of this type were used on the services from Rock Ferry Pier to Raby Mere and Heswall via Storeton and between New Ferry and Moreton Shore via Higher Bebington and Arrowe Park. It was withdrawn in 1932 when the new Leyland Cubs started to join the fleet. (Leyland Motors)
50. The relatively low floor Leyland PLSC Lion was an instant success and literally thousands were built and added to bus fleets all over the country. No.250, new in 1927, was a typical Leyland-bodied version, the attraction for the passenger being the much lower floor level achieved by means of a cranked chassis. Examples were still to be found in the Crosville fleet as late as 1949.   (Crosville)

51. Pictured below the Moreton-Upton road was contested by Crosville and Birkenhead Corporation in the 1920s. The company paid about £4,000 for the Upton end to be widened in 1921; later when Birkenhead obtained authority to run they were required to pay Crosville £2,060 which they did on 28th September 1928. An unidentified Crosville Leyland bus is seen leaving Moreton, for Upton probably about 1928 or 1929. The spire of Moreton parish church can be seen in the background and the Wallasey boundary sign, applicable from 1st April 1928, is on the left. (Valentines)

52/53/54. MacDonald & Co. built up a small but varied fleet of charabancs in the early 1920s and had garages in Birkenhead and Liverpool. The proprietor, known to his familiars as 'Harry Mac' later became a councillor for St. James' Ward. The upper picture shows a Garford charabanc B 8528, parked outside the Queen's Arms Hotel, Storeton Road, Oxton and gives a good view of the hood in the folded position. The centre picture is of a rare Rolls Royce charabanc. MacDonald took a car in settlement of a debt, scrapped the body and had a charabanc body built by Duple at Hendon. At the end of the 1920s, MacDonalds had developed their North Wales coast excursions into a regular daily service between Birkenhead and Bangor which was later extended to Liverpool and Caernarfon and the trading name Maxways was adopted. One of two Leyland Tiger TS2 coaches used on this service stands beside their Pilgrim Street garage in Birkenhead. The worker on the left was Harry Mac's father.

(TB Maund collection)

55/56/57. A new generation of buses and coaches emerged from the Leyland factory in the late 1920s and the six-cylinder single-deck Tiger and double-deck Titan were the precursors of thousands of vehicles to carry those model names. Both were much lower-built than previous vehicles and the original Titan was revolutionary in having an overall height of only 13ft which opened up the possibility of double-deck buses serving routes previously barred to them because of low bridges or overhanging trees. The low height was achieved by arranging the upper deck seats in rows of three or four with a side gangway on the offside. This intruded into the headroom of the lower saloon and a notice on each seat back on the offside advised passengers to lower their heads when leaving their seats. Despite this awkward arrangement the model was very popular. Crosville took delivery of their first TD1 Titans on 6th November 1928 and many were soon at work in Wirral. The earlier models had open staircases and No.333 is seen at the Queen's Arms Hotel, Liscard Village on the West Kirby service. Note the oval logo adopted during LMS ownership.

Centre. Crosville No.332, an open-stair Titan TD1 passes West Kirby Wirral station en route for Liscard. All the open-stair Titans were later rebuilt with enclosed rear ends.

In the lower picture a Crosville bus approaches New Ferry Toll Bar en route to Ellesmere Port or Chester and the edge of the depot in New Ferry Road can just be glimpsed. On the left can be seen the edge of the former tram depot, being converted into a combined garage and bus station for Birkenhead Corporation which dates the picture as 1932.

(TB Maund collection/TG Turner collection)

58/59. A Crosville Leyland TD5 eases its way through flood water in Market Street, Hoylake. Several of these buses were allocated to the West Kirby – Park Station and Liscard services in 1938-39. This bus, M52, has survived and is being restored to original condition by Mr H Peers.

The lower picture shows No. 368 (which later became L62 and M225) which was one of the first fully enclosed Titans. The picture dates from early 1930 as it is displaying a 'Heswall-Singleton Avenue' sign.

(IG Boumphrey collection/DS Deacon)

60/61/62. Crosville's three depots in Wirral. (Upper) West Kirby depot in Orrysdale Road with the original 1920s building on the right and the 1930s extension on the left. (Centre) Heswall bus station and typical Crosville corrugated iron-clad garage, built on land acquired with Pye's business in 1924. The bus station canopy, left, was a hazard for double-deck buses. The upper view on the opposite page shows Rock Ferry garage in New Chester Road as it was in 1952. It was opened on 1st April 1932 and solved overcrowding at other depots. This depot is now used by Crosville's successors, First Group.

(JP WillIams).

63/64. The year 1924 was the greatest for territorial expansion by Crosville and these handbills were issued to announce new services from New Ferry to Moreton and from Rock Ferry Pier to Raby Mere. Note the 6d minimum fare imposed on the latter by Birkenhead Corporation. The New Ferry-Moreton service was later extended to the Shore and was the only bus service ever to have run along Village Road, Higher Bebington. It was never resumed after suspension during the 1939-45 War. (TB Maund collection)

CROSVILLE "GREY" MOTOR SERVICES

NEW SERVICE
New Ferry to Moreton

(Toll Bar Corner)   (Plough Inn)

Commencing Wednesday, May 21st, 1924
(Unless previous notice given)

TIME TABLE and FARES until further notice.

Service No. 68   WEEK-DAYS AND SUNDAYS.

	M					S		M					S
	a.m.	p.m.	p.m.	p.m.	p.m.	p.m.		a.m.	p.m.	p.m.	p.m.	p.m.	p.m.
New Ferry (Toll Bar Corner)	10 30	1 45	3 30	5 45	7 35	9 20	Moreton (Plough Inn)	11 45	2 40	4 20	6 40	8 30	10 15
Lower Bebington (Village Road)	10 35	1 50	3 35	5 50	7 40	9 25	Upton (Eagle & Crown)	11 51	2 46	4 26	6 46	8 36	10 21
Gorsey Hey	10 40	1 55	4 05	5 57	7 45	9 30	Woodchurch (Horse & Jockey)	11 56	2 51	4 31	6 51	8 41	10 26
Higher Bebington (George Hotel or Traveller's Rest)	10 45	2 03	4 56	0 7	5 09	9 35	Half Way House Hotel	12 5	3 04	4 07	7 08	5 0	10 35
Prenton Rd. W. (Tram Term.)	10 52	2 7	3 526	7 7	5 7	9 42	Prenton Rd. W. (Tram Term.)	12 8	3 3	4 37	7 38	5 3	10 38
Half Way House Hotel	10 55	2 10	3 556	10 8	0 9	45	Higher Bebington (Traveller's Rest or George Hotel)	12 15	3 10	4 50	7 10	9	0 10 45
Woodchurch (Horse & Jockey)	11 4	2 19	4 46	198	9 9	54	Gorsey Hey	12 20	3 15	4 557	15	9	5 10 50
Upton (Eagle & Crown)	11 9	2 24	4 96	248	14 9	59	Lower Bebington (Village Road)	12 25	3 20	5	07	209	10 10 55
Moreton (Plough Inn)	11 15	2 30	4 156	30 8	20 10	5	New Ferry (Toll Bar Corner)	12 30	3 25	5	57	259	15 11 0

M—Sundays excepted.   S—Saturdays and Sundays only.

FARE LIST.

9d. 9d. 8d. 6d. 5d. 3d. 2d. 2d. New Ferry (Toll Bar Corner)
9d. 9d. 7d. 5d. 4d. 2d. 2d. Lower Bebington (Village Road)
9d. 8d. 6d. 4d. 3d. 2d. Gorsey Hey
8d. 7d. 5d. 3d. 2d. Higher Bebington (Traveller's Rest or George Hotel)
7d. 5d. 3d. 2d. Prenton Road W. (Tram Terminus)
6d. 4d. 3d. Half Way House Hotel
4d. 2d. Woodchurch (Horse & Jockey)
2d. Upton (Eagle & Crown)
Moreton (Plough Inn)

These Buses proceed from New Ferry via Lower Bebington Village, Heath Road, Gorsey Hey, Teehey Lane, Higher Bebington, Mount Road, Storeton Road, Half Way House Hotel, Woodchurch, and Upton.

Issued subject to the Company's terms, conditions, and regulations as set out in the Main Guide.

*Proprietors:—*THE CROSVILLE MOTOR CO. LTD., Crane Wharf, Chester.
Tel. 1123 Chester (2 lines).   Chars-a-bancs and Motor Buses for Private Hire.
Local Office: NEW FERRY TRAM TERMINUS BUS STATION, NEW FERRY.

5,000—21/5/24

CROSVILLE "GREY" MOTOR SERVICES

New Summer Service
ROCK FERRY (Pier) to RABY MERE
(Via NEW FERRY TOLL BAR, LOWER BEBINGTON and BROMBORO')

Commencing Wednesday, June 4th, 1924
(Unless commencement previously announced)

TIME TABLE and FARES until further notice.

Service No. 66   WEEK-DAYS AND SUNDAYS.

				S									S
	p.m.	p.m.	p.m.	p.m.	p.m.	p.m.		p.m.	p.m.	p.m.	p.m.	p.m.	p.m.
Rock Ferry (Pier)	1 40	3 04	2 06	0 7	3 08	45 9 50	Raby Mere	2 20	3 40	5 20	6 40	8 59	20 10 25
Bedford R.(New Chester R.)	1 42	3 24	2 26	27	3 28	47 9 52	Golf Pavilion	2 23	3 43	5 23	6 43	8 89	23 10 28
New Ferry (Toll Bar Cor.)	1 46	3 64	2 66	67	3 68	51 9 56	Bromboro' Station	2 25	3 45	5 25	6 45	8 109	25 10 30
Bebington Station	1 49	3 94	2 96	97	3 98	54 9 59	Bromboro' Cross	2 30	3 50	5 30	6 50	8 159	30 10 35
Lower Bebington Village	1 51	3 114	3 16	117	4 18	56 10 1	Trafalgar (Brown Cow)	2 37	3 57	5 37	6 57	8 229	37 10 42
Trafalgar (Brown Cow)	1 53	3 134	3 36	137	4 38	58 10 3	Lower Bebington Village	2 39	3 59	5 39	6 59	8 249	39 10 44
Bromboro' Cross	2 0	3 204	4 06	207	5 09	5 10 10	Bebington Station	2 41	4 1	5 41	7 18	269	41 10 46
Bromboro' Station	2 5	3 254	4 56	257	5 59	10 10 15	New Ferry (Toll Bar Cor.)	2 44	4 5	5 447	48	299	44 10 49
Golf Pavilion	2 7	3 274	4 76	277	5 79	12 10 17	Bedford R.(New Chester R.)	2 48	4 5	5 487	88	339	48 10 53
Raby Mere	2 10	3 304	5 06	308	0 9	15 10 20	Rock Ferry Pier	2 50	4 10	5 507	108	359	50 10 55

S—Saturdays only during June, July and August.

FARE LIST.

9d. 8d. 7d. 6d. 6d. 6d. 6d. Rock Ferry (Pier)
8d. 7d. 6d. 6d. 6d. 6d. Bedford Road (New Chester Road Corner)
7d. 6d. 5d. 3d. 3d. 2d. New Ferry (Toll Bar Corner)
6d. 5d. 4d. 3d. 2d. 1d. Bebington Station
6d. 5d. 4d. 3d. 2d. 1d. Lower Bebington Village
5d. 4d. 3d. 2d. Trafalgar (Brown Cow)
4d. 3d. 2d. Bromboro' Cross
2d. 2d. Bromboro' Station
2d. Golf Pavilion
Raby Mere

NOTE.—These Buses will only pick up in the Borough of Birkenhead on the Outward Journey at Rock Ferry (Pier), but will set down in the Borough on the Inward Journey anywhere by request.

The Route traversed will be via New Chester Road, Bebington Road, Bromboro' Road (Trafalgar), Old Chester Road and Allport Road

SPECIAL DAY RETURN FARE: ROCK FERRY—RABY MERE 1/3

NOTE—Ferry Single Fare Liverpool—Rock Ferry is 2½d., and the Ferry runs every 20 minutes.

Issued subject to the Company's terms, conditions, and regulations as set out in the Main Guide.

*Proprietors:—*THE CROSVILLE MOTOR CO., LTD., Crane Wharf, Chester.
Tel. 1123 Chester (2 lines).   Char-a-bancs and Motor Buses for Private Hire.
Local Office: NEW FERRY ROAD, NEW FERRY.

65/66. Crosville joined the competitive race for the London service which had been started by independent operators in 1928. Initially the service ran from Park station, travelling via Moreton, West Kirby and Heswall to Chester and then via Lichfield, Stratford-on-Avon and Oxford, using vehicles with coach seats in bus bodies. The small print states 'The coaches are driven by experienced men specially selected for this class of work and every driver is given every other day off as a rest day whilst employed on this service'.

The North Wales coast express service to Caernarfon, with its network of connecting services to Anglesey and the Lleyn peninsula, started in earnest in 1930.

(TB Maund collection)

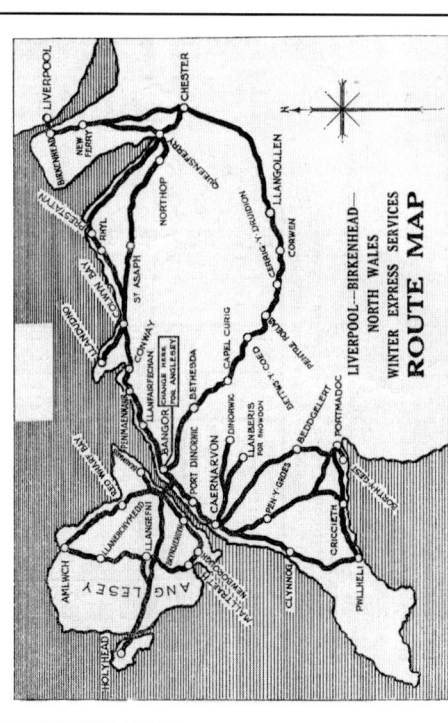

67/68. The Leyland Tiger 6-cylinder models first appeared in 1929 together with a new low-loading 4-cylinder Lion of almost identical appearance. Tiger No. 373 was delivered in 1930 and had 25 coach seats in what was a modified Leyland bus body with two outward-opening doors and a roof mounted luggage rack precariously reached by a vertical ladder at the rear. The earlier models had a very square rear end which was rounded off in later models such as this Lion seen under the canopy at Heswall bus station.
(TB Maund collection)

69. Leyland Lions and Tigers dominated the Crosville fleet during the 1930s and some soldiered on until the early 1950s. This LT2 Lion had a 32-seat Leyland body and served the company for 20 years from 1930 to 1950 being then sold for further service with the Forestry Commission. It was originally No. 396 but in 1935 Crosville adopted a system whereby an initial letter identified the model. Inexplicably every Lion variation had its own letter from A to J (except I) whereas all the Tigers, irrespective of model, were lumped together in the Ks. (A Lister)

70/71. The metamorphosis of the motor coach beyond the early charabancs is illustrated by (above) this Leyland Lioness 6 LTB1 which shared a chassis design with the Lion but was powered by the same six-cylinder engine as the Tiger and Titan. It retained the canvas roof which could be rolled back in fine weather. No. 17 was one of a pair and became K6 in the 1935 renumbering. The Tigers used on express work compared badly in appearance with the luxury coaches of competitors and, in an effort to improve it, some were repainted in the pre-war coach livery of grey and green . No. 177, below, seen here in Llandudno in 1933, had been bought new for the Liverpool-London service in 1929. It became K19 and was eventually rebodied as a bus and fitted with a Gardner diesel engine as KC19.

(TG Turner collection)

72/73/74. From 1933 onwards Crosville bought vehicles with special bodies for coaching duties, one of the first being No. 744, a Leyland Tiger TS4 with Leyland body. It was dedicated to the Liverpool-Caernarfon service and is seen unloading in Castle Square, Caernarfon at journey's end. It was renumbered K71 in 1935 and KA192 when fitted with a diesel engine in 1939.

No.965, a 1934 Duple-bodied Leyland TS4 was one of five dedicated to the London services and which originally had only 24 super-luxury seats arranged in a two-and-one formation. These were later increased to 32. It demonstrates a great leap forward in coach body design in the space of only one year. K100, a Leyland TS7, new in 1936 with Harrington body was one of four not dedicated to any particular service. The stepped waist rail was particularly eye-catching. Note the new style winged Crosville fleet name. These coaches lasted well into the 1950s. (TG Turner collection/Duple Motor Bodies/TB Maund collection)

75/76. Wirral Motor Transport Co. ran a daily summer service between Birkenhead and Bangor and, after a period of co-ordination with Crosville, sold out in February 1934. They had one AEC Regal Duple bodied coach, BG 605, which became No.980 (later T5). It was rebodied by Eastern Coachworks as a dual-purpose vehicle i.e. coach seats in a bus body and ran until 1952. It is seen in its original livery and as repainted in Crosville grey and green coach livery whilst taking part in a large private hire.

(TG Turner collection)

77/78. In December 1934 Crosville took over the business of MacDonald & Co. (Maxways) together with 10 modern AEC Regal coaches which carried the names of Welsh castles. They continued as coaches for five years and were then rebodied as buses by Eastern Coachworks. BG 614, originally with a Massey Bros. body, was numbered T11 and remained in service until 1952.

(TB Maund collection/R Marshall)

79/80. Many of the PLSC Lions suffered from body rot attributed to being washed by high pressure hoses and a rebodying programme was carried out in the early and mid-1930s. The replacement Eastern Coachworks bodies were very attractive but the retention of the short PLSC radiator always gave these buses an old fashioned look. The early Lions came in two lengths, the 25ft PLSC1 which became class A, and the 27ft 6in PLSC3 which was class B. A22 and B37 are seen here with their new bodies at Rock Ferry depot and Meols Drive, West Kirby respectively. The difference in length is clear

(A Lister/TG Turner collection)

81. The cover of a comprehensive leaflet issued by Crosville on the extension of the services terminating at New Ferry to Woodside on 1st August 1930. A similar brochure was issued to mark the extension of the Heswall and Parkgate routes terminating at Singleton Avenue and Prenton tram terminus to Woodside on 1st Octobner 1930.

(TB Maund collection)

CROSVILLE MOTOR SERVICES

REORGANISATION AND EXTENSION OF

CHESTER—NEW FERRY SERVICES

VIA ELLESMERE PORT AND RHOSMORE ROAD
AND VIA
LITTLE SUTTON DIRECT

-- TO --

BIRKENHEAD (WOODSIDE)

Commencing on FRIDAY, AUGUST 1st, 1930.

REVISED TIME TABLES & FARE LISTS.

ALSO SUMMARY TIME TABLES BETWEEN
CHESTER ELLESMERE PORT VIA WHITBY
AND
BIRKENHEAD ELLESMERE PORT
VIA POOLTOWN ROAD AND HOOTON PARK.

**Through Fares from Eastham to Liverpool
(Landing Stage) via 'Bus and Boat.**

Return Tickets issued by Crosville Motor Services or Birkenhead Corporation Motors between Eastham and Allport Road, Bromborough to Birkenhead and Liverpool are available for the Return Journey on either of the respective Services.

Proprietors: CROSVILLE MOTOR SERVICES Ltd.,
HEAD OFFICE: CRANE WHARF CHESTER.

82. In 1930 Alfred Harding participated in a Birkenhead-London service with George Taylor of Chester, both running as 'All British Line' but Harding soon withdrew as loadings were poor, Taylor continuing alone. Two of these normal-control Albions were bought second-hand from Scotland for this service.

(Harding's [Wirral] Ltd.)

83. Two Harding's coaches are seen on New Brighton promenade in the late 1930s trying to attract customers for local tours. At this time they were painted green and cream.
(Hardings (Wirral) Ltd)

84. After the 1939-45 War, Hardings operated a number of works contracts and this ex-Ribble double-deck coach was acquired for this purpose. It is seen at the entrance of Harding's garage at the top of Exmouth Street, the site of present day Yates' Wine Lodge. The end of Oliver Street is visible in the background.
(TG Turner)

85/86. All sorts of odd vehicles were taken over by Crosville with small businesses and many of therm could be seen at Rock Ferry depot from time to time. The Dennis Ace was popular with small operators. It was known as the Flying Pig because of its protruding bonnet and, surprisingly, this was the only one to join the Crosville fleet. W21 came from S.Williams & Sons of Pentre Broughton, a business taken over by the company in June 1936 and ran until 1949. There were many Crosville Bedfords and S3 came from J R Lloyd of Bwlchgwyn in 1938, continuing to run for Crosville until 1950.

(A Lister)

87/88. The Leyland Titan TD1 double-deckers with Leyland low height bodywork were to be seen in the Crosville fleet for over 20 years. L3 (formerly No.20) was a 1931 model and is seen at Chester destined for Birkenhead via Ellesmere Port; it demonstrates the company's strange preference for 'Widd board' destinations (named after the firm who supplied them) rather than use a screen which could be wound on which was the usual method. Most of the petrol-engined TD1s were later fitted with diesel engines and thereby moved into the M class, L3 becoming M199. After rebodying in 1947, it ran until 1953. In 1938 destination screens were fitted but only to double-deckers and the KA class of Leyland Tigers. Some of the displays were abbreviated to the extent that a stranger would understandably be puzzled e.g. E.PORT B'HEAD. M216 (a 1930 model formerly 355 and L49) is seen so equipped in Beckwith Street, the Birkenhead Park station loading point. It gave 23 years' service. (T G Turner collection)

89/90. {Upper) Leyland Titan L63 was new in 1929 to Brookes Bros. White Rose Motor Services of Rhyl whose business was taken over in 1930. It is seen in Greasby on a special Saturday afternoon duplicate journey between Wood Lane and West Kirby. It continued in service until 1952, still with its petrol engine. (Lower) After the 1939-45 War, the very centralised Tilling Group to which Crosville belonged from 1942, decreed that as many buses as possible would be fitted with the enormous destination equipment shown and adopt service numbers. Crosville concurred rather reluctantly, M167 (formerly 57 and L19) a 1931 TD1, being seen in Chester Street, Birkenhead on a hospital special to Cleaver Sanatorium, Heswall. Even this has been unnecessarily abbreviated . (J Crutchley/J P Williams)

91/92/93. Crosville had many lightly loaded services using narrow country roads and the Leyland Cub range, introduced in 1931 was ideal for these duties. N6 (formerly 665) was a short-wheelbase KP2 model new in 1932 seating 20 passengers and thereby could be legally worked by only one man. N76-7 (986-7) were new in 1934 and used the longer KP3 chassis seating 26 passengers. They were regularly used on the Birkenhead-Chester via Rivacre, Stoak & Stanney and Heswall-Banks Road services. Small buses comprised 15% of the Crosville fleet and when war increased the passenger demand many were too small. N6 was sold to the RAF in 1942.
(A Lister/TG Turner collection/A Lister)

94. The narrow Pasture Road railway bridge at Moreton station was hazardous for traffic and was rebuilt in 1937. The bus is a Leyland Lion LT7 No. H6, new in 1935 and is working the New Ferry-Moreton Shore service. Note the small domes on the back of the bus which denoted the Division and depot to which the bus was allocated. (TG Turner collection)

95. A long forgotten facility was the post-box carried by late evening trams and buses to provide a late collection. Leyland Titan TD3 M8 (922), new in 1934, stands in Chester Market Square waiting departure to Woodside via Ellesmere Port. Control staff had to take care that a bus fitted with the necessary bracket to hold the post-box was allocated to the advertised journeys   (TG Turner collection)

96/97. A rare picture of the tide causing problems for the driver of 1934 Leyland Titan TD3 M6 (920) as he nears the Parkgate terminus of the service from Birkenhead via Thornton Hough. This contrasts with a peaceful scene west of Moreton Cross with 1936 Leyland Titan TD4 M46 heading for West Kirby.
 (TG Turner collection/Valentines)

98/99. The traditional method of building a bus body was to use a wooden frame until the mid-1930s when bodybuilders started to experiment with metal-framed bodies. Leyland's attempt, typified by the shallow V- front was plagued by corrosion problems. They were numbered M13-21 and one of them is seen at Woodside in 1948 in the company of a bus bought second-hand from Sheffield to boost the post-war double-deck fleet while M18 (below) is seen when new in 1935.

(J Manly/TG Turner collection)

100/101. The smooth lines of the Eastern Counties bodies on the 1933-34 Leyland TD3s contrasted very favourably with the earlier TD1 and TD2 models with traditional Leyland 'piano fronts'. M5 (919) loads at Woodside on the Chester direct service while M12 (936) has had a rather serious contretemps with a Morris 8 on the Heswall via Pensby route.

(C Routh/RL Wilson collection)

102. A popular excursion in the 1930s was between Merseyside and Llandudno using the daily summer sailings of the Liverpool & North Wales Steamship Co. in one direction and Crosville coaches in the other. Passengers were obliged, on arrival at Llandudno, to notify the tours office of their intended mode of return. The cost was eight shillings (40p).

(TB Maund collection)

t Summer Issue.   ⚊ 1934 ⚊   P B 4i.

MERSEYSIDE
TO
LLANDUDNO
COMBINED ROAD AND STEAMER SERVICES

BY ARRANGEMENT BETWEEN
CROSVILLE MOTOR SERVICES LTD.;
THE LIVERPOOL & NORTH WALES STEAMSHIP CO. LTD
C.C. 1/320.   C.C. 1/332.   C.C. 1/337.

Commencing SATURDAY, MAY 19th, 1934
and continuing until the termination of the Steamer Services on Monday, September 24th, 1934.
WEEKDAYS AND SUNDAYS (Bank Holidays excepted).
OUT BY STEAMER AND RETURN BY COACH (OR VICE VERSA).

NORTH WALES STEAMER.
LIVERPOOL (Princes Stage) dep. 10 45 a.m. | LLANDUDNO (Pier) - dep. 5 15 p.m
LLANDUDNO (Pier) - arr. 1 5 p.m | LIVERPOOL (Princes Stage) arr. 7 30 p.m.
COACHES DEPART AND ARRIVE AS FOLLOWS:—

		a.m.	a.m.	
LIVERPOOL (Pier Head, Mann Island)	dep.	—	—	
BIRKENHEAD (Woodside)	,,	—	10 30	
WALLASEY (Seacombe Ferry)	,,	9 25	—	
LLANDUDNO (Coach Station, Oxford Rd.)	arr.	1 20 p.m.	1 0 p.m.	
		p.m.	p.m.	
LLANDUDNO (Coach Station, Oxford Rd.)	dep.	6 0	6 30	Passengers returning to
BIRKENHEAD (Woodside)	arr.	8 35		Liverpool must pay their own
WALLASEY (Seacombe Ferry)	,,	—	10 25	Ferry Fee of 2d. from
LIVERPOOL (Mann Island)	,,	—		Birkenhead

RETURN FARE from LIVERPOOL, BIRKENHEAD or WALLASEY
BY STEAMER **8/-** OR COACH
AVAILABLE DAY OF ISSUE ONLY.

S.S. St. TUDNO.
For Conditions of Booking and Offices see overleaf.

357. 5M. 6/34 G.R.G. Ltd.

---

103. The KA class of Leyland Tiger TS7 single-deck buses with 32-seat Eastern Coachworks bodies with cutaway roof over the bonnet began to appear in large numbers in 1937. They had a hard war and, in 1950, several including KA21 seen here en route to Brimstage on the New Ferry-West Kirby service, were rebuilt in 1950 to lengthen their lives, the last being withdrawn in 1960.

(TG Turner)

104. The Leyland TD5 double-deckers with Eastern Coachwork low bridge bodies were placed in service in 1938-40, substantial numbers being allocated to West Kirby depot. The rear view is of M55, new in 1938.

(I Kennedy)

105. The AEC Q side-engined double-decker with single wheels on the rear axle was well ahead of its time and, although many single-deckers were built, only 23 double-deckers were put into service. This vehicle was demonstrated to Crosville in 1933 just as they had made an agreement to run a Liverpool-Garston service for the Corporation for five years. It made a great contrast with Edwardian trams and when the Corporation took over in 1938 it was transferred to Rock Ferry depot running on Ellesmere Port and Chester services. It seated 60 passengers but, being non-standard, was used mainly at peak hours. It was successively numbered 1000, L87 and L68 and was withdrawn in 1945.

(TB Maund collection)

106/107. The 1939-45 War had a profound effect on Crosville. Industries in Wirral and its immediate environs were expanded and many essential factories and government departments were evacuated to what were seen as areas safe from aerial bombing in North Wales and rural Cheshire. The increased demand for bus services placed a great strain on a company whose fleet comprised 15% of small vehicles with no more than 26 seats and only 15% double-deck buses which became more and more in demand. Sixteen buses intended for Southdown Motor Services Ltd. of Brighton were diverted to Crosville and most ran in Chester and Wirral. These were full height Park Royal-bodied Leyland TD7 double-deckers with a central gangway upstairs, the first buses of the seating arrangement to enter the Crosville fleet since the Leviathans. M122 loads for Chester at Woodside. Another of the batch, M118 is seen after being fitted with Tilling destination indicators loading at the same place. These buses were always recognisable by their alien GCD (Brighton) registrations.

(JP Williams/J Manly)

108. Manchester Corporation had taken delivery of many new buses just before the war to replace trams but some of the trams were retained or reinstated to save fuel. No fewer than 37 Manchester Leyland TD1 buses were hired to Crosville for varying periods between 1940 and 1946 and this one is seen on the Birkenhead-Mold service.

(RL Wilson collection)

109. A40, seen at Rock Ferry depot, was one of five Leyland 1928 PLSC3 Lions bought from Ribble Motor Services Ltd. In 1940. Its fleet number was a mistake as the A series was for the shorter PLSC1 model and it was soon renumbered B40. It is seen still in Ribble livery and served Crosville for 10 years being then sold to the Forestry Commission for further service.

(TB Maund collection)

A careless man, Ezekiel Clowne
He would not keep his torchlight down!
He flashed it in the Driver's face,
Really a most regrettable case.
Ezekiel now will never see
The brave New World that's going to be

LOOK OUT IN THE BLACKOUT

CROSVILLE

110. During the war, Crosville ran a series of press advertisements about safety in the blackout. The rhymes are said to have been written personally by the general manager, W J Crosland Taylor.

(TB Maund collection)

111/112. During the war Crosville hired many vehicles but at the end of hostilities many of the owners wanted them back, causing serious problems for the company. The solution was to buy up as many old double-deck buses as possible and, between 1946 and 1950, Crosville bought 101, the oldest dating from 1929 and the majority from the early 1930s with Leyland TD1s in the majority. The company's works at Sealand Road, Chester did a magnificent job bringing these elderly veterans up to standard, fitting them with the new Tilling indicators and, in some cases, rebodying them. M515 (HL 5339) was one of a pair which came from the West Riding Automobile Co. of Wakefield in 1946 with petrol engines and centre-entrance Roe bodies. They were fitted with diesel engines before entering service with Crosville and rebodied by Eastern Coachworks in 1949. L131, a 1931 AEC Regent, seen below at West Kirby, came from Plymouth Corporation via Bristol Omnibus Co. as late as 1949. Its original Ransomes body was scrapped and the body shown was taken off a Crosville TD1 which was rebodied by Eastern Coachworks.   (RF Mack/JP Williams)

113. Seen in Rock Ferry depot yard are L79 a 1932 Leyland TD2 with Mumford body acquired by Crosville in 1945 from Plymouth Corporation. It was later fitted with a diesel engine and renumbered M235, being sold in 1954. Alongside is an original Crosville 1931 TD1, successively numbered 55, L17 and M167, which was rebuilt by Eastern Coachworks in 1945 and also ran until 1954. (TG Turner collection)

114. End of season. A line up of delicensed buses at Rock Ferry depot at the end of the 1950 season. All but the furthest one are petrol-engined and date from the early 1930s. (J Crutchley)

115. One of the youngest second-hand buses acquired was this 1936 Metro-Cammell-bodied Leyland TD4c, new to Chesterfield Corporation. The c in the type designation denoted fitment of a hydraulic torque-converter, a type of transmission which Crosville spurned and a normal gearbox was fitted before entering service with the company. M516 is seen in Heswall depot yard.

(RF Mack)

116. This lonely 1949 scene, looking towards Birkenhead, is unrecognisable today being the main bus stop serving Clatterbridge Hospital. The bus, which is en route to Parkgate, is a 1933 Leyland TD2, one of the last to carry the 'piano front' style of body, which successively carried the numbers 795, L86, L67 and M229.

(J Crutchley)

117. In an endeavour to get more life out of some diesel-engined 20-seat 1937 Leyland Cubs, a number were selected in 1950 for conversion by Beadle to integral 35-seaters, using the engines, transmission and radiators. In general the rebuilds were not successful and this one, PC13 (originally P13), seen at West Kirby on the Park Station via Saughall Massie service, was later fitted with a Perkins 4.7 litre engine.   (JP Williams)

118. The Tilling Group's standard post-war double-deck bus was the Bristol K with Eastern Coachworks bodywork and Crosville received a large allocation from 1946 onwards. MB282 was a 1947 K6B, denoting the fitment of a Bristol 6-cylinder engine. Withdrawal of these buses started in 1960.
(TB Maund collection)

119. The Tilling post-war single-deck bus was the Bristol L rear-entrance 35-seater. Pictured on a private hire in Liverpool is KG132, a K6G Gardner-engined model new in 1950. Beside it is SL66, a 1950 29-seat Bedford coach with Duple body. (JP Williams)

120. Many of the rebodied buses bore a strong resemblance to the new Bristols, especially if the old fashioned short radiator was replaced by the longer CovRad radiator which was specially manufactured for this purpose. This was a 1932 Leyland TD2, originally No.735 then L76 and M30. Its new Eastern Coachworks body was fitted in 1949 and it was withdrawn in 1956, its body being transferred to a Bristol K6A. (H Peers)

121. Clash of the Titans. An unfortunate coming together of Crosville TD5 M120, one of those diverted from Southdown in 1940, and a Wallasey Corporation PD1 in the Haymarket, Birkenhead in June 1948. (TG Turner collection)

122/123. The immediate pre-war Leyland TD5s received some body attention, including the fitment of Tilling indicators. Note the elimination of the upper and lower cream bands to facilitate more economical spray painting . M56 is seen at Woodside on the Chester Direct service while M99 (below) rests in West Kirby depot yard.
   (T B Maund collection/H Peers)

124. A line up of buses in Heswall depot yard. The bus on the right was second-hand from Bolton Corporation. From the right the buses are M234, M52, M80 and M83 (fifth one unknown) The use of the number 114 for all the Birkenhead-Heswall routes (originally 114, 114A, 114B) was an absurdity which was not eliminated until routes were renumbered in 1959.

(TG Turner collection)

125. Epitaph. This picture of Leyland TD1 M159 (ex-47, L9), new in 1931 and outwardly in original condition, was taken at Woodside on the last Sunday that TD1s were in service, 27th September 1953.

(TG Turner)

126/127. Many coaches which would have been considered time-expired in normal times had to be kept in service until deliveries of new vehicles caught up after the war. K32 (originally 374) was a 1930 Leyland Tiger TS2 which originally had a coach-seated Leyland bus body. It was rebodied by Eastern Coachworks in 1937 and continued in service until 1952. It is seen in the post-war green and cream coach livery.

By contrast, Bristol LL6B coach KW231 is seen in company with another of the type on the London service. These 1951 Eastern Coachworks-bodied 35-seaters were known as 'Queen Marys' and were described by the general manager of Crosville, W J Crosland Taylor, as 'the most comfortable coaches we have ever run'.

(TB Maund collection/J P Williams)

128. One of the least known Crosville services from Wirral ran on visiting days to Burntwood Sanatorium and KB40, a 1947 Bristol L6A, powered by an AEC engine, is seen leaving the Raven Hotel, Prees Heath after a refreshment halt. After withdrawal in 1960, this bus became a mobile shop for St. Helens Co-op.
(TG Turner)

129. A 1932 Leyland Lion LT5, F4 (751) was photographed in Heswall depot yard in February 1951, shortly before withdrawal in company with S4, a Beadle-bodied 28-seat Bedford OB bus, new in 1947. These Bedfords, fitted with 6-cylinder petrol engines, were bought as a stop gap when new buses were hard to come by and were withdrawn in 1953-54. At Heswall it was used on the Banks Road local service.
(JP Williams)

130. This Leyland TS4 coach K203 had an interesting history having been purchased in 1932 as a 26-seat coach (643). It was rebodied as shown by Burlingham in 1940 but sold to Wilts & Dorset Motor Services of Salisbury in 1941 to help with their massively increased traffic on Salisbury Plain. In 1947 it was bought back and ran until 1953. It is seen at Liverpool Pier Head in 1950 preparatory to crossing to Birkenhead on a North Wales express service. (J P Williams)

131. Post-war legislation permitted buses to be 8ft wide instead of 7ft 6in and Crosville generally fitted wider seats to give greater comfort. MW471 was a 1952 Bristol KSW6 and is pictured at Woodside bound for Loggerheads during a time when Crosville decided that the ultimate destination of the bus should be shown on the lower rather than the upper destination indicator. Note the complete absence of shelter for waiting passengers. (T B Maund collection)

132. Crosville, having been allocated several full height double-deckers in 1940, knew the benefits of the type and started to turn away from the low bridge models as far as possible as their upper deck seats for four were very unpopular. MW434 with Eastern Counties high bridge body was new in 1952 and is seen a few years later with the train shed of Woodside railway station in the background. The original triple destination screens have been reduced to two and the upper and lower cream bands have been eliminated. (R F Mack)

133. The old and the new. Leyland Tiger TS7 KA84, new in 1937 is seen at Rock Ferry depot in 1959 shortly before sale; it had a body rebuild in the company workshops in 1950. Alongside is EMG345, a 1958 dual-purpose 41-seat Bristol MW6G, representative of the growing number of underfloor-engined single-deckers in the fleet (T G Turner)

134. The Bristol Lodekka was a revolutionary design for double-deck buses, the transmission being arranged to the side of the chassis so that there was a virtually flat floor, This enabled the upper deck seats to be arranged in pairs and at the same time retain the low height necessary to clear low bridges and trees. DFG164 was a 60-seater new in 1964. Note the grilles for the patent Cave-Browne-Cave ventilation and heating system. The bus is on the Parkgate stand against a background of Woodside railway station. Note the crude wartime shelters, proof only against vertical rain.
(J P Williams)

135/136/137. Rock Ferry depot was Crosville's largest Wirral property and also the Divisional Headquarters of an area which included Liverpool. This late-1960s bird's eye view of the yard shows a good selection of Lodekkas, a few single-deck buses and Bristol Ks and three modern coaches. The bus wash is at the rear of the yard and in the lower picture Lodekka DFB107, a 1960 model, is being cleaned. The final picture (opposite) shows the interior of the garage with a 1960 Bristol MW6G coach and a new RELH6G 47-seat coach CRG578. The small panels beneath the waistline read 'Crosville Liverpool London Service' and were illuminated at night.
(T G Turner collection)

138/139. The Lodekka design lent itself to use as a medium distance coach, its low centre of gravity giving a smooth and comfortable ride. Eight of these Bristol LD6Bs entered service on the Liverpool-North Wales express services in 1954; they had seats for 52 passengers, straight staircases and luggage racks above the rear wheel arches. Until the old Conway bridge was eliminated they could not travel beyond Llandudno. This was ML677 (later DLB677), pictured middle; the coach type destination indicators were later replaced by the bus type and all eight were eventually downgraded to bus duties.

Their replacements were ten forward-entrance Bristol Lodekka FLFs, delivered in two batches in 1963 and 1964. They seated 37 passengers on the upper deck and only 18 in the lower saloon, the remaining space being given over to luggage. DFB113 is seen below leaving Skelhorne Street bus station, Liverpool in 1963 en route to Caernarfon, the mediaeval obstruction at Conwy having been by-passed by this time.

(T B Maund collection/R L Wilson)

ACKNOWLEDGEMENTS

The author is indebted to many friends who have made pictures available for this book and extends apologies to any who, inadvertently, have not been mentioned by name.
Especial thanks go to Mr TG Turner of Wallasey and the Exors. of RL Wilson of West Kirby.
The late DS Deacon, a former Crosville executive, made a number of pictures available before his death.
Thanks are due to the staff of Wirral Libraries and the Unilever Port Sunlight archive for making certain documents available over the years.
The JF Parke Memorial Library of the Omnibus Society at Coalbrookdale kindly made available copies of various timetables for copying.

BY THE SAME AUTHOR:

The Tramways of Birkenhead & Wallasey	(with M Jenkins), Light Rail Transit Association 1987
The Birkenhead Railway	Railway Correspondence & Travel Society, 2000
Merseyrail Electrics, the Inside Story	NBC Books, PO Box 1225, Sheffield SIO 4YJ, 2001
Mersey Ferries Volume 2	(with M. Jenkins), Black Dwarf Publications, 2003

BY THE SAME PUBLISHERS:

Yesterday's Wirral No. 3 - West Kirby & Hoylake
Yesterday's Wirral No. 4- Wallasey, New Brighton & Leasowe
Yesterday's Wirral No. 5 - Wallasey, New Brighton & Moreton
Yesterday's Wirral No. 6 - Neston, Parkgate & Heswall including Thurstaston & Irby etc.
Yesterday's Wirral No. 7 - Birkenhead, Oxton & Prenton including Bidston & Upton
Yesterday's Wirral No. 8- Bebington & Mid Wirral Villages
Yesterday's Wirral No. 9 - Ellesmere Port to Bromborough
Yesterday's Wirral   - Port Sunlight 1888 - 1953 - Ian Boumphrey & Gavin Hunter
Yesterday's Wirral   - Pictorial History 1890 - 1953
Birkenhead at War 1939 - 45
Railway Stations of Wirral - Mersey Railway History Group
Plus many more – for a FREE catalogue of over 40 books mainly about Wirral - written, published or distributed by the publishers - contact

Ian & Marilyn Boumphrey 'The Nook' 7 Acrefield Road
Prenton Wirral CH42 8LD
Tel/Fax: 0151 608 7611
e-mail: ian@yesterdayswirral.co.uk
or visit our website: www.yesterdayswirral.co.uk